AND YOGHURT RECIPES

compiled by
Astrid Bartlett

SALMON

Index

Banana Yoghurt Smoothie   40
Beef Curry   24
Broccoli, Stilton & Brie Soup   11
Cauliflower, Broccoli, Cheese
            & Tomato Bake   47
Cheese Pudding   46
Cheese Scones   39
Cheese Straws   6
Cheese, Tomato & Bacon Flan   45
Cheese & Tomato Bread   35
Cheesey Leek Bake   19
Cheesey Yorkshire Pudding   22
Cheshire Cheese Pasta Bake   23
Chilled Avocado Soup   37
Christmas Scones   32
Cottage Cheese Tart   42
Derby Pancakes   27
Ewes' Milk Cheese & Cherry Tomato Pie   5

Exmoor Blue Cheese
            Vegetable Gratin   30
Garlic Cheese Dip   29
Garlicky Mushroom Ramekins   38
Gratinated Potatoes   16
Grilled Brie & Walnuts   3
Lasagne   13
Leek, Bacon & Cheese Tart   15
Lemon Cheesecake   31
Macaroni Cheese   34
Quick Pasta   18
Rock Cakes   14
Savoury Pancakes   26
Smoked Mackerel Paté   21
Soda Bread   8
Spinach Soup   43
Sweet 'n' Savoury Meringues   7
Yoghurt Fruit Scones   10

Cover *front:* Cottager Milking   *back:* Bringing home the Milk *by William Shayer Snr.*
title page: Feeding the Calf *by K. Stuhlmuller*

Printed and Published by J. Salmon Ltd., Sevenoaks, England © Copyright

Grilled Brie & Walnuts

We are encouraged to "eat British" and "eat local" and this tasty cheese spread can be made with home-produced Somerset Brie or with ewes' milk or any local soft cheese.

1½ lb Brie or similar soft cheese **1 teaspoon Dijon mustard**
1 teaspoon butter **1 oz approx. chopped walnuts**

In a bowl, cream together the butter and Dijon mustard and then spread the mixture over the top of the whole piece of cheese. Put the cheese on a flameproof dish and place under the grill, about 6 inches below the grill, for 3 to 4 minutes until the cheese begins to bubble. Remove from the grill and sprinkle the cheese with chopped walnuts. Return to the grill for about a further 2 minutes until the nuts are golden, but take care not to burn them. Serve spread on crusty granary rolls, chunks or slices of French bread or on slices of toast.

Ewes' Milk Cheese & Cherry Tomato Pie

If Little Ryding or Shepherd's Crook soft cheeses are not available, use Somerset Brie or Camembert instead, though the finished result will not be quite the same.

1 lb puff pastry   A soft ewes' milk cheese
12 approx. cherry tomatoes (or 6 big tomatoes halved)
A handful of freshly snipped chives   Black pepper   1 egg, beaten

Set oven to 425°F or Mark 7. Butter a baking sheet. Roll out the pastry on a floured surface to an approx. 10 inch square. Scatter some of the chives in the centre of the pastry, place the whole cheese on top and surround it with tomatoes, and finish with some on top. Scatter the rest of the chives on to and around the cheese and tomatoes and grind over some black pepper. Brush the edges of the pastry with beaten egg and lift up the diagonal corners to meet over the centre of the cheese. Press together and seal by crimping the edges. Transfer to the baking sheet and bake for about 20 to 25 minutes until the pastry is puffed and golden. As an alternative, try torn basil leaves instead of chives. Serves 4.

Cheese Straws

Cheese straws are ideal for nibbles for parties and look festive when twisted into spirals. Try making a few hoops out of the mixture and then feeding some straight straws through them to look like sheaves of corn.

8 oz plain flour
A pinch of English mustard powder
A pinch of Cayenne pepper
A few twists of freshly ground
  black pepper

A pinch of salt
5 oz butter, softened
4 oz Cheddar cheese, finely grated
2 egg yolks
Juice of ½ large lemon

A little cold water

Set oven to 400°F or Mark 6. Butter a baking sheet. Sift the flour and dry seasonings together into a bowl and rub in the butter until the mixture resembles breadcrumbs. Mix in the grated cheese, add the egg yolks and lemon juice and mix all well together, adding a little water if necessary to bind. Knead into a ball in the bowl for a few minutes and then roll out to about ¼ inch thickness on a floured surface. Cut into strips, twist them into spirals and arrange on the baking sheet. Any left-over dough can be made into miniature biscuits. Bake for about 10 minutes until the straws are golden brown and crisp. Allow to cool before handling as they can be fragile.

Sweet 'n' Savoury Meringues

Do not waste the egg whites from making cheese straws but turn them into these miniature, filled 'party' meringues.

2 egg whites   4 oz caster sugar

FILLING

¼ pint pot double cream   A pinch of Cayenne pepper
A small pinch of salt   A little finely grated Cheddar cheese

Line a baking sheet with silicon paper (or butter well). First whisk the egg whites in a bowl until they reach soft peaks and remain in the bowl when it is turned upside down. Continue whisking, adding the sugar a little at a time, until the mixture holds stiff peaks. Spoon teaspoonsful of the mixture on to the baking sheet and cook very slowly in a very cool oven until the meringues are firm to the touch. When cold remove from the baking sheet. To make the filling, whisk the cream until stiff and carefully fold in the pepper, salt and cheese. Use the mixture to sandwich together pairs of meringues to make an unusual and delicious party snack. The filling mixture can also be used to top little cheese biscuits.

Soda Bread

This is one of the simplest of all bread recipes. Just mix the ingredients, lightly knead to shape – there's no waiting time for it to rise – and you have a delicious fresh loaf in under an hour. Soda bread is best eaten fresh, within 24 hours, as it quickly goes stale. Traditionally it would have been made every day.

14 oz plain strong flour	**7 oz natural yoghurt**
2 teaspoons bicarbonate of soda	**4 fl. oz milk**
1 teaspoon salt	**1 teaspoon runny honey**

Set oven to 400°F or Mark 6. Grease a baking sheet. Sift the flour, bicarbonate of soda and salt into a bowl. Make a well in the centre, pour in the yoghurt, milk and honey, and knead lightly together with the hands. Turn out on to a lightly floured surface and shape into a round. Transfer to the baking sheet, cut a cross into the top of the loaf with an oiled sharp knife and bake for about 30 to 35 minutes until golden brown and the base sounds hollow when tapped. Transfer to a wire rack and cover with a clean tea towel to retain the moisture.

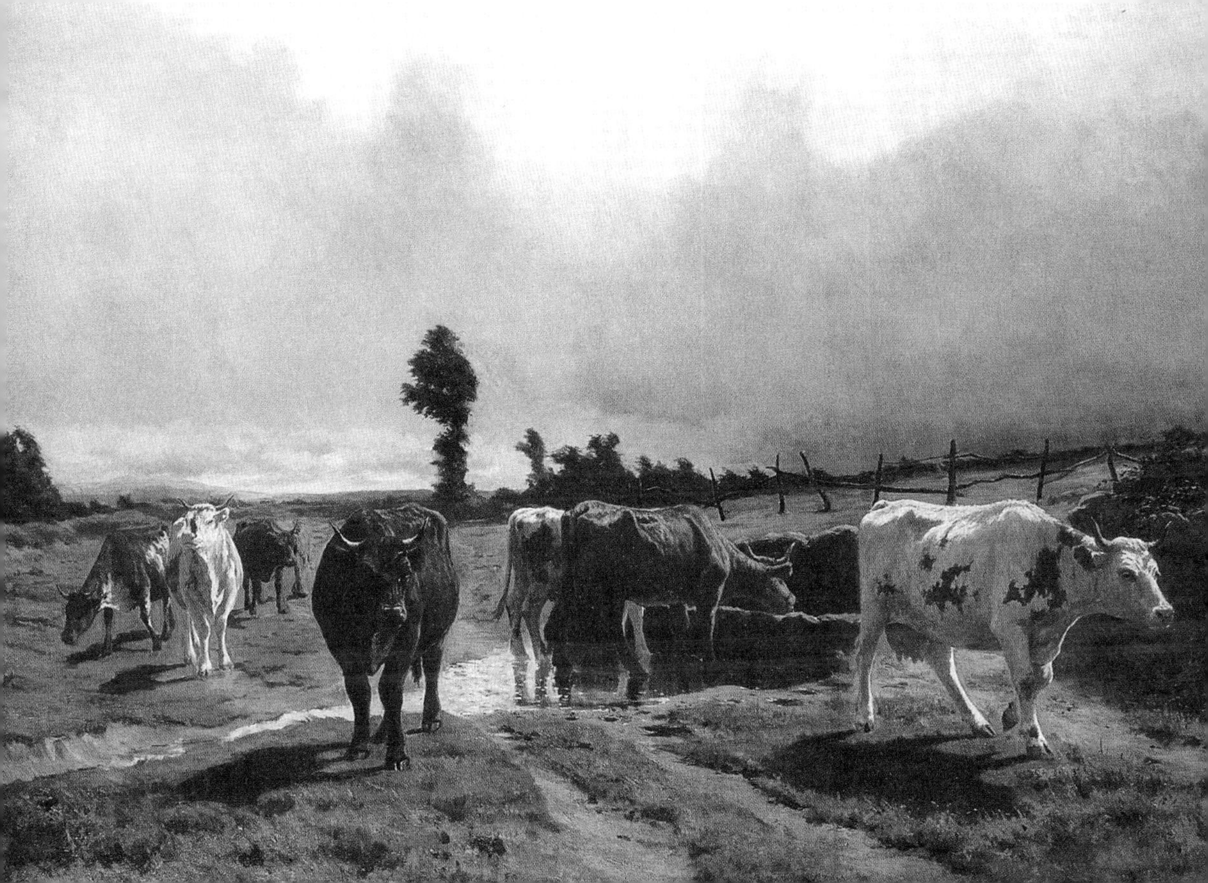

Yoghurt Fruit Scones

In the days before refrigerators, milk would often go sour in the summer. Our ancestors discovered that soured milk made better scones than those made with fresh milk. This recipe, which uses yoghurt instead of sour milk, produces even lighter, moister scones which should in theory, last longer in store – if they weren't so popular with the family.

8 oz self-raising flour   **2 oz caster sugar**
Pinch of salt   **4 oz mixed dried fruit**
2 oz butter, softened   **3 tablespoons yoghurt**

Set oven to 400°F or Mark 6. Butter a baking sheet. Sieve the flour and salt into a bowl, rub in the butter and mix in the sugar and the dried fruit. Add the yoghurt and knead into the mixture with the hands until it is a firm but pliable dough. Roll out to about 1 inch thickness on a floured surface and cut into circles with a pastry cutter (or a tumbler). Arrange on the baking sheet and bake for about 7 to 10 minutes until risen and lightly browned. Makes about 8 to 10 scones.

Broccoli, Stilton & Brie Soup

If preferred, a soft ewes' milk cheese may be used instead of Somerset Brie.

3 oz Stilton cheese	1 leek, cut into 1 inch lengths
3 oz Somerset Brie	2 heads broccoli
A little olive oil	1½ pints chicken stock
1 large onion, roughly chopped	Freshly ground black pepper
2 cloves garlic, crushed	Yoghurt to swirl

Parsley sprigs to garnish

Heat the olive oil in a large saucepan, add the onion, garlic and leek and cook gently until soft. Wash the broccoli and cut into lots of miniature heads. Add to the saucepan and continue cooking for a little longer. Pour in the chicken stock and a few twists of black pepper. Bring to the boil and simmer until the broccoli is tender. Crumble the cheeses, add to the soup and allow them to melt but do not let the soup boil. Give the soup a stir. Serve piping hot, adding a swirl of yoghurt in each bowl and a sprig of parsley for garnish, accompanied by freshly baked, crusty wholemeal bread. Serves 6.

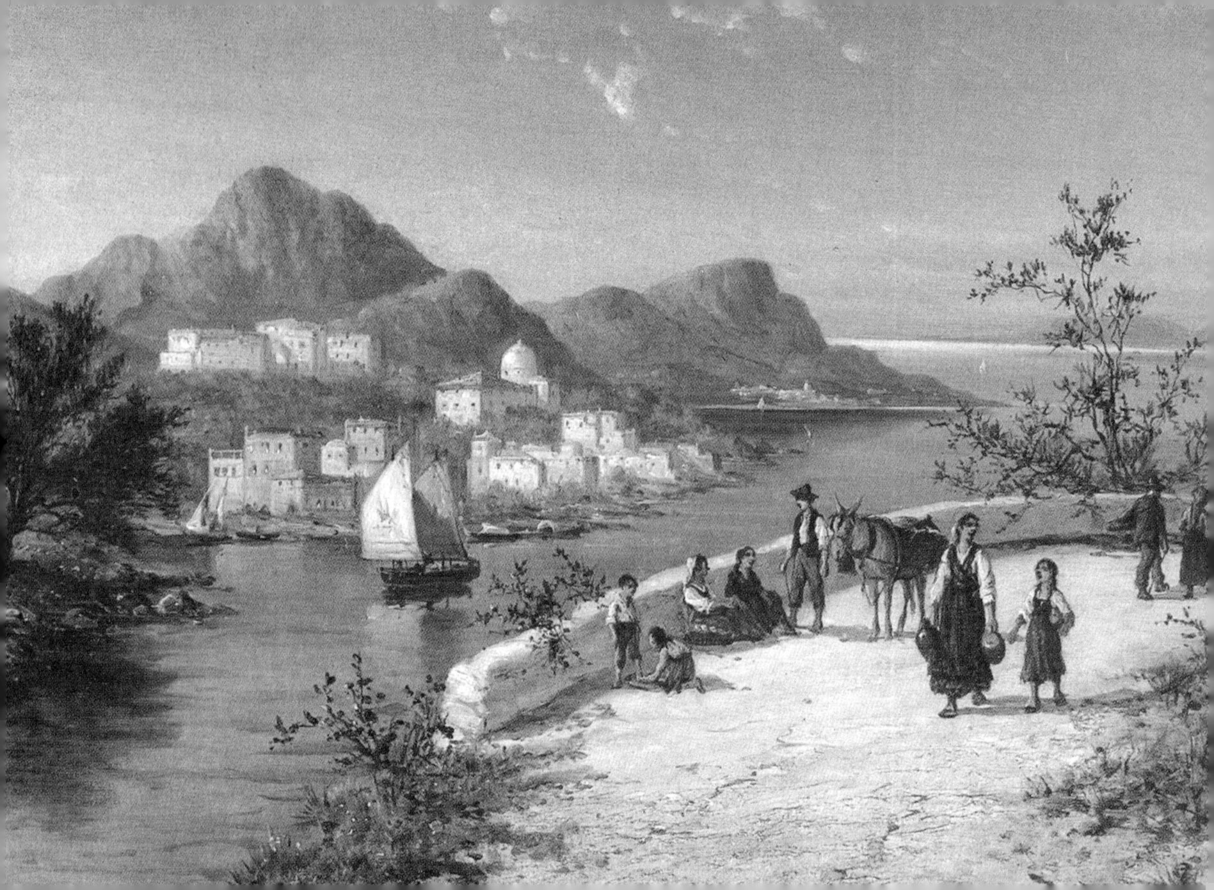

Lasagne

For a really substantial and satisfying meal, this dish is hard to bea.

**1 lb fresh minced beef   A knob of butter   1 large onion, chopped   1 clove garlic,
1 red, green or yellow pepper, diced   8 oz tomatoes, skinned and chopped
1 beef stock cube and boiling water   ¼ pint red wine   Freshly ground black peppe⸱
Pinch dried mixed herbs   Cornflour for thickening   2-3 oz Cheddar cheese, grated
A few sheets of lasagne   Grated Parmesan cheese for topping**

SAUCE: 2 oz plain flour   2 oz butter   1 pint milk

Set oven to 375°F or Mark 5. Butter an ovenproof lasagne dish. Melt a knob of butter in a large pan and cook the onion, garlic and pepper until transparent but not brown. Add the mince, cook to brown it and stir well. Add the chopped tomatoes. Melt the stock cube in boiling water and add to the dish with the red wine. Add a few twists of black pepper and the herbs, and stir well. If necessary, thicken with a little slaked cornflour. Make the sauce. Melt the butter in a pan, cook for 1 minute then stir in the milk a little at a time, stirring continuously over a low heat until thickened. Stir in the grated Cheddar cheese. Line the base of the dish with a layer of meat mixture, cover with a few sheets of lasagne and then some of the sauce. Repeat the layers until all the ingredients are used up, finishing with white sauce. Top with grated Parmesan cheese. Bake for about 30 minutes until browned on top. Serves 4.

Modena, Italy by William Dommerson

Rock Cakes

As an alternative flavouring to lemon zest, try mixed spice or, if preferred, omit either and have them plain. If no yoghurt is available, use a little milk as a substitute.

8 oz plain flour
1 teaspoon baking powder
3 oz butter, softened
2 oz sugar
4 oz currants or mixed dried fruit
Pinch of salt (optional)
Grated zest of ½ lemon
1 egg, beaten
3 tablespoons yoghurt

Set oven to 400°F or Mark 6. Butter a baking sheet. Sift the flour and baking powder into a mixing bowl then rub in the butter until the mixture resembles breadcrumbs. Add the remaining dry ingredients and the lemon zest, and mix to a stiff dough with the beaten egg and yoghurt. Spoon small heaps of the mixture on to the baking sheet and bake near the top of the oven for about 10 to 15 minutes until golden. Transfer to a wire rack to cool.

Leek, Bacon & Cheese Tart

A tasty light lunch or supper dish. Leek and bacon are made for each other.

**4 oz bacon rashers, trimmed and cut into 1 inch strips
3 leeks split lengthways, and cut across into 1 inch pieces
A little olive oil   2 oz butter   2 oz plain flour   1 pint milk   Black pepper
8 pared slices Cheddar cheese and a few gratings
2 tomatoes cut into wheels   Basil or oregano to garnish**

DOUGH: 8 oz self-raising flour   A pinch of salt   2 oz butter, softened   ¼ pint milk

Set oven to 375°F or Mark 5. Butter a 9 inch flan dish. Heat the olive oil in a large saucepan and cook the bacon and leek pieces until tender. Remove and set aside. Melt the butter in the same pan, add the flour, cook for 1 minute then gradually add the milk, stirring continually until the sauce thickens. Season to taste. Return the bacon and leek to the pan and stir in. For the base, sift the flour and salt into a bowl, rub in the butter and then mix in the milk to produce a soft dough. Roll out to about ¼ inch thickness on a floured surface and use to line the flan dish; trim the edge. Prick all over with a fork and bake blind for 5 minutes. Remove the flan from the oven, spoon in the bacon/leek sauce, spread out, and arrange the cheese slices and tomato wheels on top. Bake for 35 to 40 minutes until the base is cooked and the top is browned. Garnish with cheese gratings and torn basil or oregano. Serves 4 to 6.

Gratinated Potato

Thick and creamy ewes' milk yoghurt and sliced potatoes are the basis for this versatile dish which goes with so many other foods. It has plenty of flavour but doesn't overwhelm the meals it accompanies..

About 6 medium potatoes, washed or peeled, and sliced
1 pint milk   1 bayleaf   Salt   1 clove of garlic, crushed
Freshly ground black pepper
1 pot thick and creamy ewes' milk yoghurt
A little cornflour   6 oz Cheddar cheese, grated   Grated nutmeg

Set oven to 375°F or Mark 5. Butter an ovenproof gratin dish. Put the sliced potatoes in a saucepan with the milk, add the bayleaf and a little salt, and cook for about 5 minutes. Remove the potatoes with a slotted spoon, arrange a layer in the dish, sprinkle over some crushed garlic, and season with pepper. Then build up, layer by layer until all the potatoes and garlic are used up. Remove the bayleaf from the cooled milk in the pan and mix in the yoghurt, with a little slaked cornflour to prevent separation. Reheat the milk and yoghurt gently, whisking all the time until it thickens. Pour over the potato slices and top with grated cheese and freshly grated nutmeg. Bake for about 1 hour until golden brown on top and the potatoes are soft. Serves 4 to 6.

Stable Companions by Eugene Maes

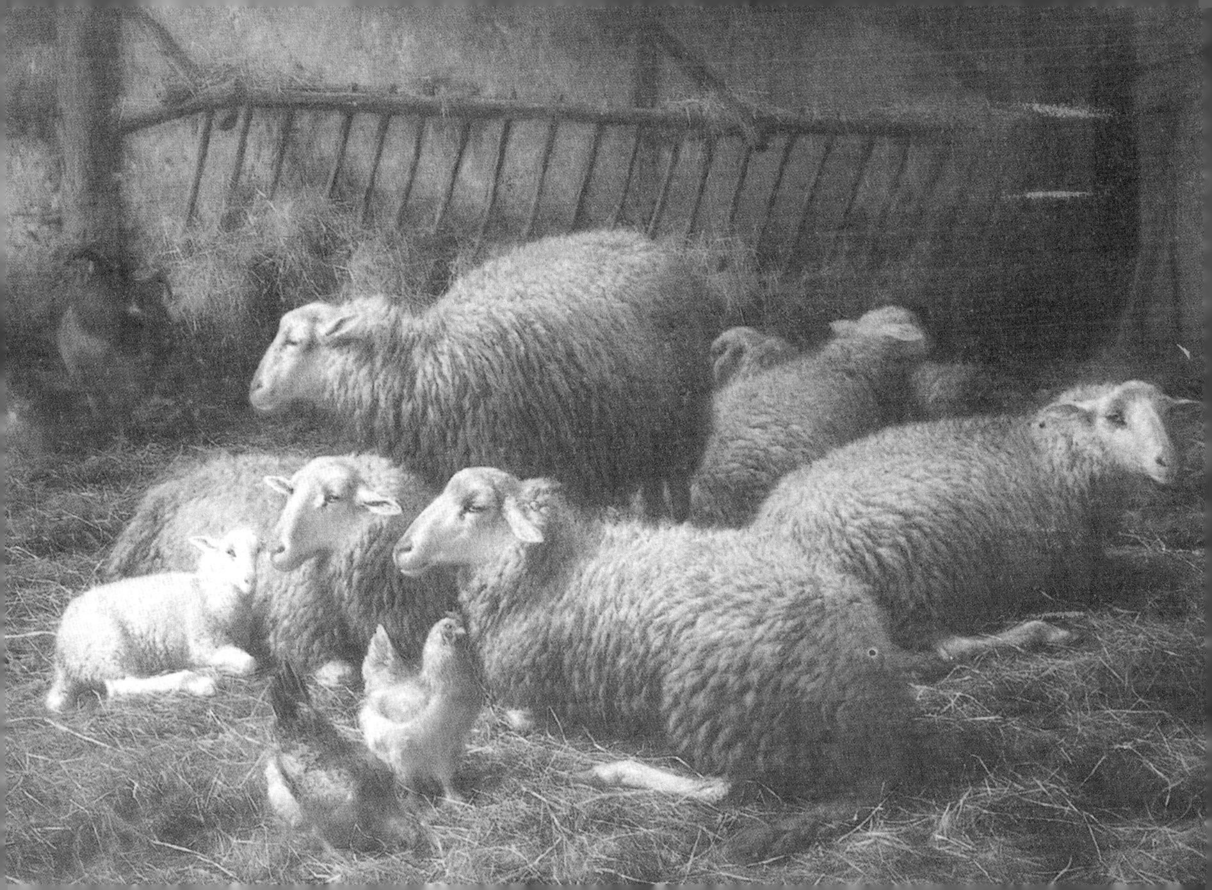

Quick Pizza

Milk can be used instead of yoghurt for making the base; and try altering the topping ingredients to suit your fancy. For example, anchovies, black olives, pineapple etc.

SCONE BASE

**6 oz self-raising flour   Pinch of salt   2 oz butter, softened
2-3 tablespoons yoghurt**

TOPPING

**A little pesto sauce   6 tomatoes, quartered   2-3 oz Cheddar cheese, grated
A bunch of chives, snipped   Salt and black pepper**

Set oven to 400°F or Mark 6. Butter a pizza dish. First make the scone base. Sift the flour and salt into a bowl, rub in the butter and stir in the yoghurt to make a dough. Roll our roughly to a circle about ½ inch thick, on a floured surface, and transfer on to the pizza dish. Prick all over with a fork and bake blind for about 5 minutes. When cooked, remove from the oven and assemble the topping. Spread pesto sauce over the scone base. Put the quartered tomatoes, the grated cheese and the snipped chives into a bowl and stir together. Tip the mixture over the base and spread out. Season with salt and freshly ground black pepper. Bake for about 10 minutes until the cheese melts all over the tomatoes. Serves 4.

Cheesey Leek Bake

Soft cheese, yoghurt and grated Parmesan make a delicious, creamy sauce to cover the leeks for this popular lunch or supper dish.

8 young leeks   2 eggs
About 6 ozs soft ewes' milk cheese
5 tablespoons yoghurt   2 ozs grated Parmesan cheese
Salt and freshly ground black pepper
1 oz fresh breadcrumbs

Set oven to 375°F or Mark 5. Well butter an ovenproof dish. Trim the leeks, cut in half and slit lengthways and wash really well under cold running water. Put into a saucepan, cover with water, bring to the boil and simmer for about 5 minutes until just tender. Drain well and arrange in the dish. In a bowl, beat the eggs with the soft cheese, the yoghurt and 1oz of the grated Parmesan cheese. Season well. Spoon the mixture over the leeks. Mix the remaining grated Parmesan with the breadcrumbs and sprinkle over the dish. Bake for about 30 minutes until crisp and golden. Serves 4.

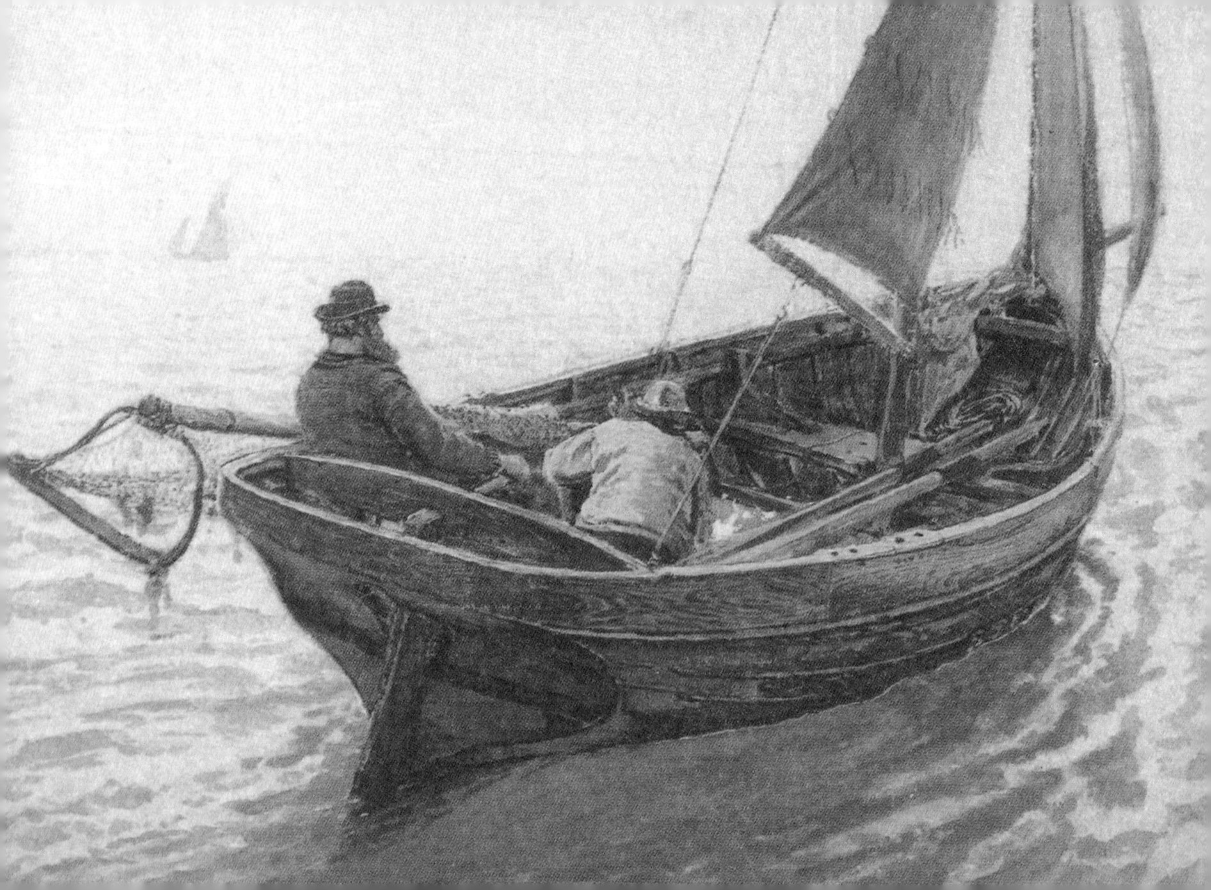

Smoked Mackerel Paté

*This paté makes a delicious starter served with Melba toast,
or nibbles for parties spread on little cheese biscuits.*

**3-4 smoked mackerel fillets   6 oz full fat soft cheese (or strained yoghurt)
A few generous twists of black pepper   Lemon juice**

Remove the skin from the mackerel fillets. For a rustic paté, break up the flesh of the fish into a bowl with the fingers, and then mash the soft cheese into it. For a more refined, smoother paste, put the fish and cheese into a food blender and whiz together. Then add the black pepper and lemon juice to taste, and mix in well. Cover the bowl with cling film and leave in the refrigerator until required. For a special occasion, cut strips of smoked salmon, spread with paté and roll up. Arrange on a plate with a squeeze of lemon juice and some freshly ground black pepper. Garnish with a sprig or two of fresh dill or a sprinkle of dried dill.

Soft cheese can be made at home by straining some ewes' milk yoghurt through a muslin cloth overnight. Put the yoghurt in the middle of the cloth, pull up and knot the corners and suspend all night over a bowl to catch the whey. Next morning, scrape the cheese from the cloth, put it into a bowl and mash in a little salt.

Off to the Fishing Grounds by Charles Hemy

Cheesey Yorkshire Puddings

Either make one big pudding using a roasting tin or a dozen bun-size puddings using a patty pan or multiple bun tray.

4 oz plain flour
1 egg, beaten
½ pint milk
A little butter
About 12 small cubes Cheddar cheese

Set oven to 425°F or Mark 7. Sieve the flour into a bowl, make a well, add the egg and milk and beat well to a thick batter. If time allows, leave the batter to stand for a while in a cool place, before using. Put knobs of butter into the roasting tin or individual tins and place in the oven to get really hot. When hot, remove from the oven, drop cubes of cheese into the tin or tins, pour in the batter and return to the oven. Bake near the top of the oven until well risen and golden brown.

Cheshire Cheese Pasta Bake

Crumbly white Cheshire cheese is ideal for cooking. Any shaped pasta can be used.

4 oz approx. pasta   1 onion, roughly chopped   2 cloves garlic, crushed
A little butter   A little olive oil   A few broccoli florets   A few chives, snipped

SAUCE: 2 oz butter   2 oz plain flour   ¼ pint milk

Set oven to 350°F or Mark 4. Butter a deep ovenproof dish. Melt some butter in a large saucepan and cook the onion and garlic until soft but not brown. When cooked, remove from the pan to the dish and set aside. Reserve the saucepan with its juices. In another saucepan, bring some water to the boil and add the pasta. Cook for about 5 minutes. Drain the part-cooked pasta, return to the pan, pour over a little olive oil and swirl around to prevent it sticking. In a third pan, cook the broccoli in a little water until bright green, then remove from the heat. Make the sauce. Using the first saucepan, melt the butter in the remaining juices over a low heat, stir in the flour then gradually add the milk stirring continually. Now add sufficient of the broccoli water to make a medium thick sauce. Add the snipped chives, salt and pepper, and the cooked onion and garlic. Now add the pasta and the drained broccoli with the chopped tomatoes and stir well. Spoon the mixture into the dish and top with crumbled Cheshire cheese. Bake for about 15 to 20 minutes until the cheese is melted and the dish is heated right through. Serves 4.

Beef Curry

This curried beef stew is delicious served with basmati rice, a selection of pickles and chopped green salad, together with cucumber, tomato, banana, apples and peppers etc.

**2 lb chuck steak, cubed   A little olive oil   A knob of butter
Freshly ground black pepper   2 large onions, chopped
2-3 cloves garlic, crushed   2 teaspoons crushed coriander
1 teaspoon crushed cumin   ½ teaspoon freshly ground cardamom
2 inch piece fresh root ginger, grated
4 tablespoons ewes' milk yoghurt or thick and creamy Greek yoghurt
A little water   Salt as necessary   A little cornflour for thickening**

Heat the olive oil and butter in a large saucepan, sprinkle the meat with freshly ground black pepper and brown all over in the pan. When brown, remove and set aside in a warm dish. Put the onion in the pan and cook for about 5 minutes. Next, add the garlic and spices, return the meat to the pan and gradually stir in the yoghurt and water. Add salt as preferred. Cover the pan with a lid and simmer very, very gently for about 2 hours, stirring occasionally. When cooked, if the sauce seems too thin, thicken with a little slaked cornflour. Cornflour will help to stabilise the yoghurt if it has a tendency to curdle. Serves 6 to 8.

Twenty-Four   To Summer Pastures by Joseph Adams RSA

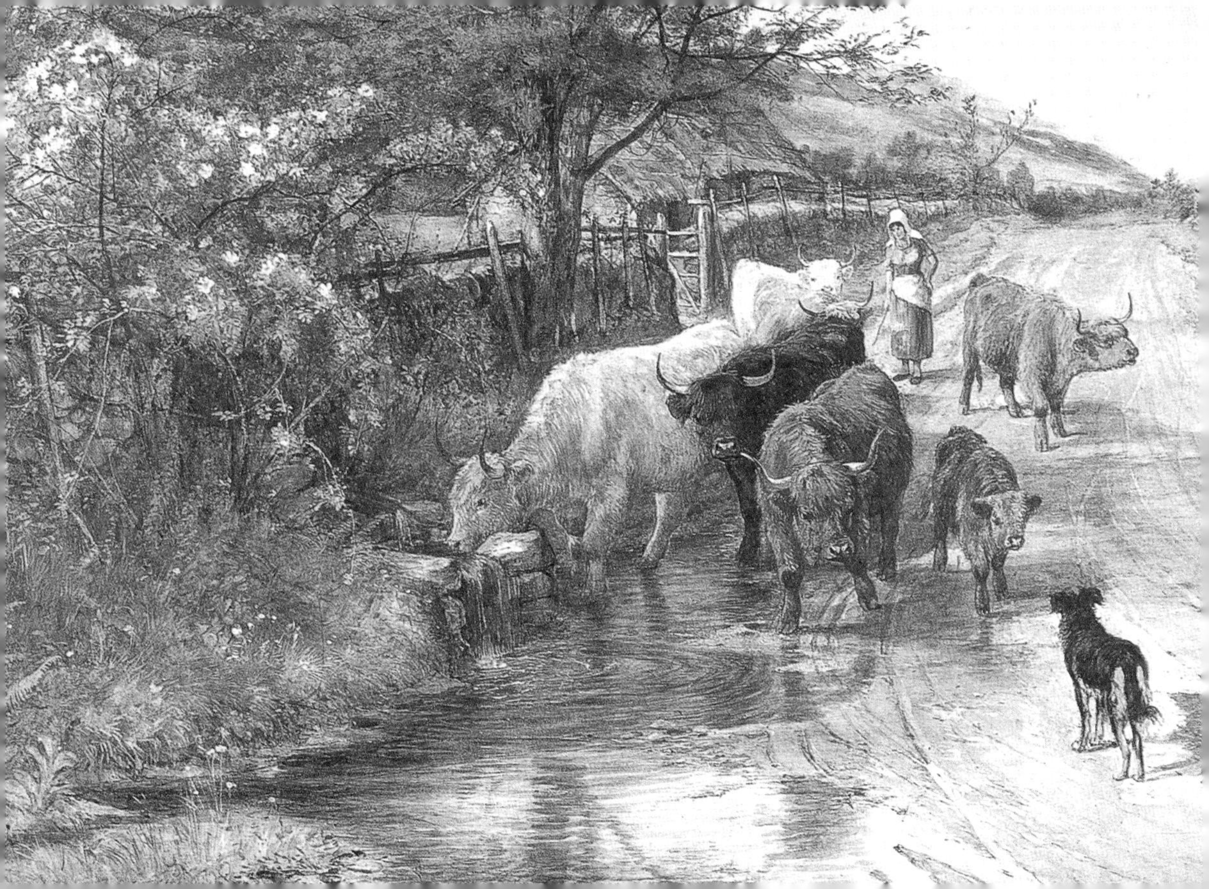

Savoury Pancakes

These cheese and chive pancakes make a tasty snack or a light lunch served with salad and fresh rolls. They even taste good when cold.

4 oz plain flour	**2-3 oz Cheddar cheese, grated**
½ pint milk	**A few fresh chives, snipped**
1 egg, beaten	**A walnut of butter**

Sieve the flour into a mixing bowl, add half the milk and the beaten egg and mix well. Beat in the remaining milk to make a smooth batter. In another bowl, mix together the grated cheese and snipped chives. Melt a knob of butter in a small (7 inch) frying pan and, when hot, spoon in sufficient batter and swirl it round to cover the base of the pan thinly. When the underside is lightly browned, turn the pancake over, sprinkle a centre strip with the cheese and chive mixture and fold in the edges to cover the filling. Continue cooking until the cheese begins to melt; serve on a hot plate. Makes about 8 to 10 pancakes.

Derby Pancakes

This dish is packed with the goodness of spinach, cheese and tomatoes. Derby and Derby Sage are close-textured cheeses made from cows' milk, which develop a fuller flavour as they mature..

8 plain pancakes (see page 26)	¼ pint tomato juice
Cooked spinach	A sprinkle of oregano
9 oz Derby cheese, grated	Salt and pepper
1 lb tomatoes, skinned	2 oz fresh breadcrumbs

Set oven to 400°F or Mark 6. Well butter an ovenproof dish. First make the plain pancakes; these can be made in advance and kept in the refrigerator or frozen, if desired. Cook a few handfuls of spinach in a little water, drain well and chop roughly. Spread cooked spinach over each pancake, use 6 oz of the Derby cheese to sprinkle over the spinach, and roll up the pancakes. Arrange the pancakes in the dish. To skin the tomatoes, plunge them in boiling water and peel, then chop them roughly and mix with the tomato juice. Add a sprinkling of oregano, season with salt and pepper and pour the tomato mixture over the pancakes. Mix the remaining grated cheese with the breadcrumbs and sprinkle over the tomatoes. Bake for about 20 minutes until browned on top. Serves 4.

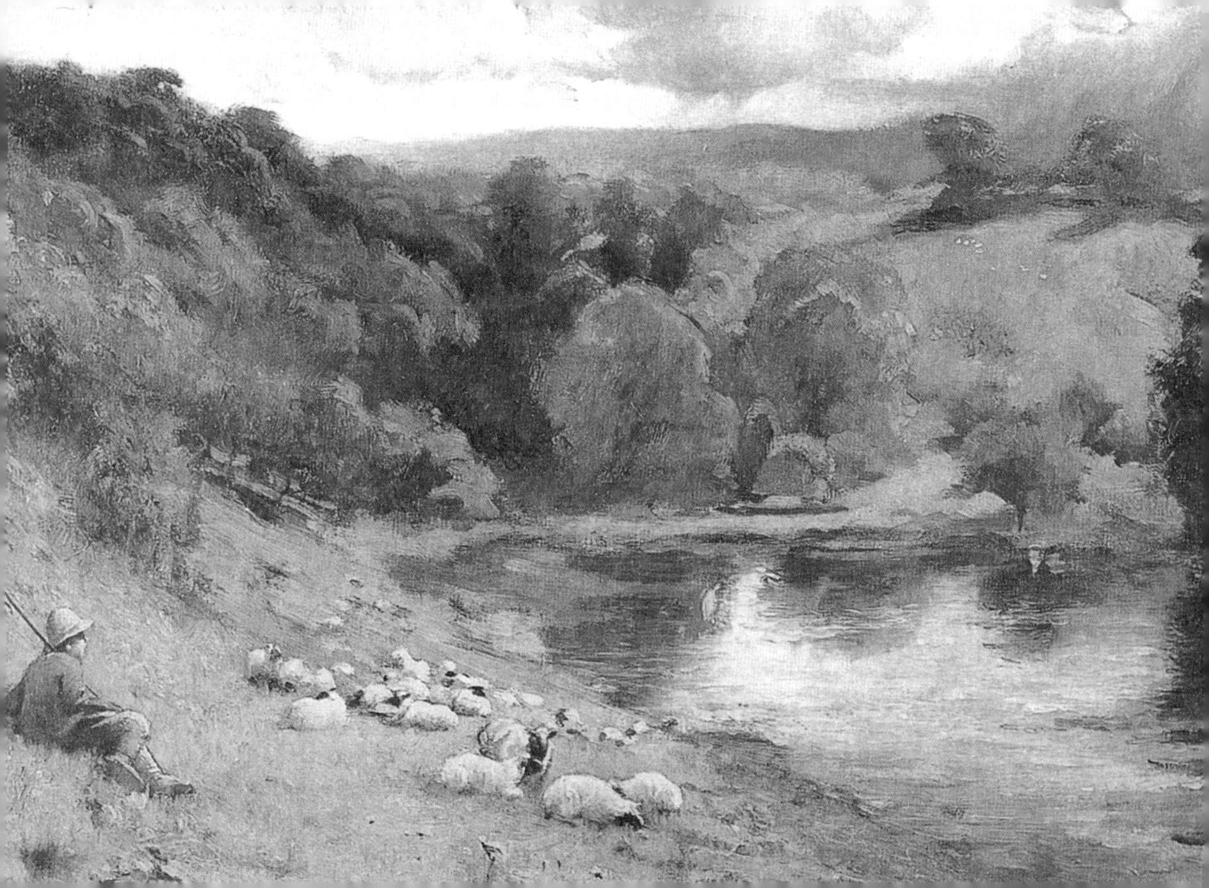

Garlic Cheese Dip

Cheese dips are easy to make. This dip uses garlic as its main flavour, but other suggestions are prawn, curry, chive, basil, spring onion, aubergine pickle, sweetcorn, pineapple etc; experiment with ingredients, flavours and textures.

6 oz Cheddar cheese, grated
5 fl.oz ewes' milk yoghurt or thick, creamy Greek yoghurt
2 tablespoons mayonnaise   1 clove garlic, crushed
1 tablespoon chopped fresh parsley   Freshly ground black pepper
Paprika pepper for sprinkling   Sprigs of parsley for garnish

Put the grated cheese into a bowl with the yoghurt and mayonnaise, the crushed garlic and chopped parsley and a few twists of black pepper. Stir all in well together. Spoon the mixture into a pretty serving dish, sprinkle with paprika pepper and garnish with sprigs of parsley. Serve with fresh vegetables such as slices of carrot, cauliflower florets and celery sticks. Alternatively, offer small robust cheese biscuits, large potato crisps, bread sticks or pieces of French bread.

The Young Shepherd by Lance Calkin ROI

Exmoor Blue Cheese Vegetable Gratin

If Exmoor Blue cheese is unavailable, then Stilton makes a good substitute for this cheesey, simple to make lunch or supper dish.

1 lb potatoes	**A good knob of butter**
1 lb carrots	**A bunch of spring onions**
1 lb parsnips	**6 oz Exmoor Blue cheese**

Set oven to 375°F or Mark 5. Butter a fairly large ovenproof dish. First wash and peel the vegetables and cut them into thick slices. Put all the vegetables into a saucepan, cover with water, bring to the boil and cook for about 8 to 10 minutes until tender. Drain and set aside. Melt the butter in the pan. Chop the spring onions and cook them lightly in the butter for about 2 minutes, just to soften. Put the drained vegetables into the pan with the onions and stir around until they are all lightly covered with butter. Spoon the vegetables into the dish, slice the cheese and arrange on top of the vegetables. Bake for about 20 minutes until the cheese is melted and bubbling. Serves 6.

Lemon Cheesecake

This recipe uses rather a lot of bowls, but it is worth it in the end. Limes can be substituted for lemons and lime jelly comes out a very pretty colour.

BASE

8 oz digestive biscuits, crushed   2 oz butter   2 level tablespoons golden syrup

TOPPING

1 block lemon jelly   Juice and zest of ½ lemon
8 oz plain cottage cheese, sieved   3 oz caster sugar
½ pint double cream

Butter a 9 inch flan dish. Put the biscuits into a polythene bag and crush to small crumbs with a rolling pin. Melt the butter in a pan with the syrup and then tip in the crumbs. Remove the pan from the heat and mix together. Tip the mixture into the flan dish, spread out and press down well. Melt the jelly with the smallest amount of boiling water necessary and leave to cool. Grate the lemon zest into a bowl, add the squeezed lemon juice and combine with the jelly. Sieve the cottage cheese into another bowl, add the sugar and beat well together. Whisk the cream until stiff and add to the cottage cheese mix. When the lemon jelly is cool enough, combine it into the cottage cheese mixture. Stir really well together, then spoon the mixture on to the biscuit base and spread out evenly. Put into the refrigerator and leave until set. Serves 6 to 8.

Christmas Scones

These scones are a good treat to make at Christmas, using up any left-over mincemeat from the mince pies.

8 oz self-raising flour
2 oz butter, softened
4 oz mincemeat
2 heaped tablespoons ewes' milk yoghurt

Set oven to 375°F or Mark 5. Butter a baking sheet. Sieve the flour into a mixing bowl and rub in the butter. Mix the mincemeat with the yoghurt and add to the flour/butter mixture. Gently knead the mixture with the hands to produce an even dough. Roll out to about 1 inch thickness on a floured surface and cut out into circles with a pastry cutter (or a tumbler). Arrange on the baking sheet and bake for about 8 to 10 minutes until risen and golden brown. Transfer to a wire rack to cool. Makes about 8 to 10 scones.

The Holly Seller by Birket Foster RWS

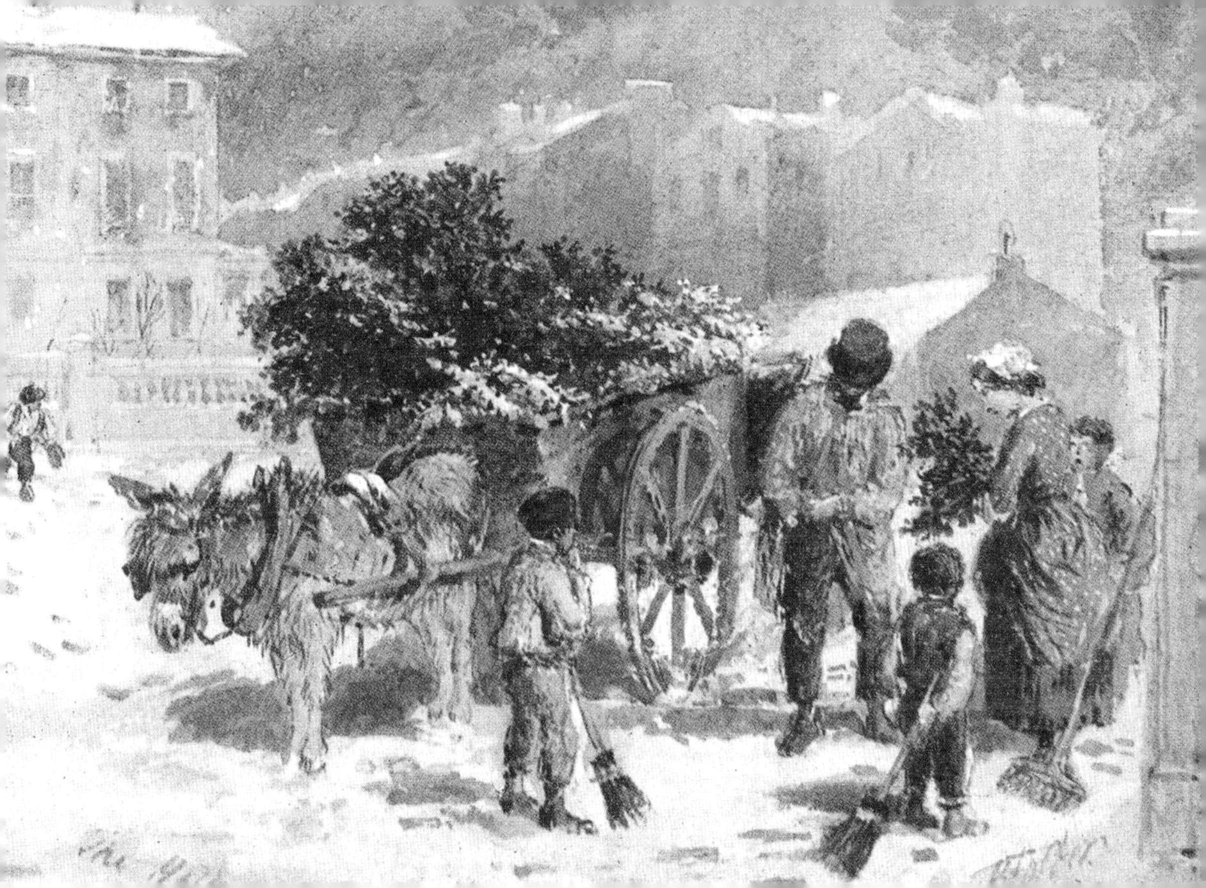

Macaroni Cheese

This is a straightforward macaroni cheese recipe with chives to give it piquancy and a topping enhanced by the subtle flavours of the oriental spices.

4 oz approx. dried macaroni   A knob of butter   6 rashers streaky bacon
1 onion, roughly chopped   6 tomatoes, quartered   4 oz Cheddar cheese, grated
A handful of porridge oats   A sprinkling of curry powder   A few snipped chives

SAUCE

2 oz plain flour   2 oz butter   1 pint milk   Freshly ground black pepper

Set oven to 400°F or Mark 6. Butter a deep ovenproof dish. Cook the macaroni for about 8 to 10 minutes in a pan of salted water. Meanwhile, melt a knob of butter in a saucepan and cook the bacon and onion until tender. Transfer the bacon and onion to the dish. Using the same saucepan to add to the flavour, make the white sauce. Melt the butter, stir in the flour and cook for 1 minute. Slowly add the milk a little at a time and stir continuously over a low heat until thickened. Add a few twists of black pepper. Drain the macaroni and add, with the quartered tomatoes, to the bacon and onion in the dish, pour over the white sauce and mix thoroughly. Put the grated cheese, oats, curry powder and snipped chives into a bowl, mix with the hands and sprinkle over the contents of the dish. Cook for about 20 minutes until browned on top and heated right through. Serves 4.

Cheese and Tomato Bread

A rich, moist savoury loaf that is quick and easy to make.

**9 oz self-raising flour   1 teaspoon baking powder
4 eggs   2 tablespoons oil
2 tablespoons tomato purée
5 oz strong Cheddar cheese, grated
6 sun-dried tomatoes, chopped
1 tablespoon fresh basil leaves, chopped
Salt and pepper**

Set oven to 350°F or Mark 4. Butter and line a 1 lb loaf tin. Sift the flour and baking powder into a mixing bowl. Beat in the eggs, oil and tomato purée. Stir in the rest of the ingredients and season well. Spoon the mixture into the tin, smooth the top and bake for about 45 minutes until the loaf is cooked through and a skewer inserted comes out clean. Turn out on to a wire rack to cool.

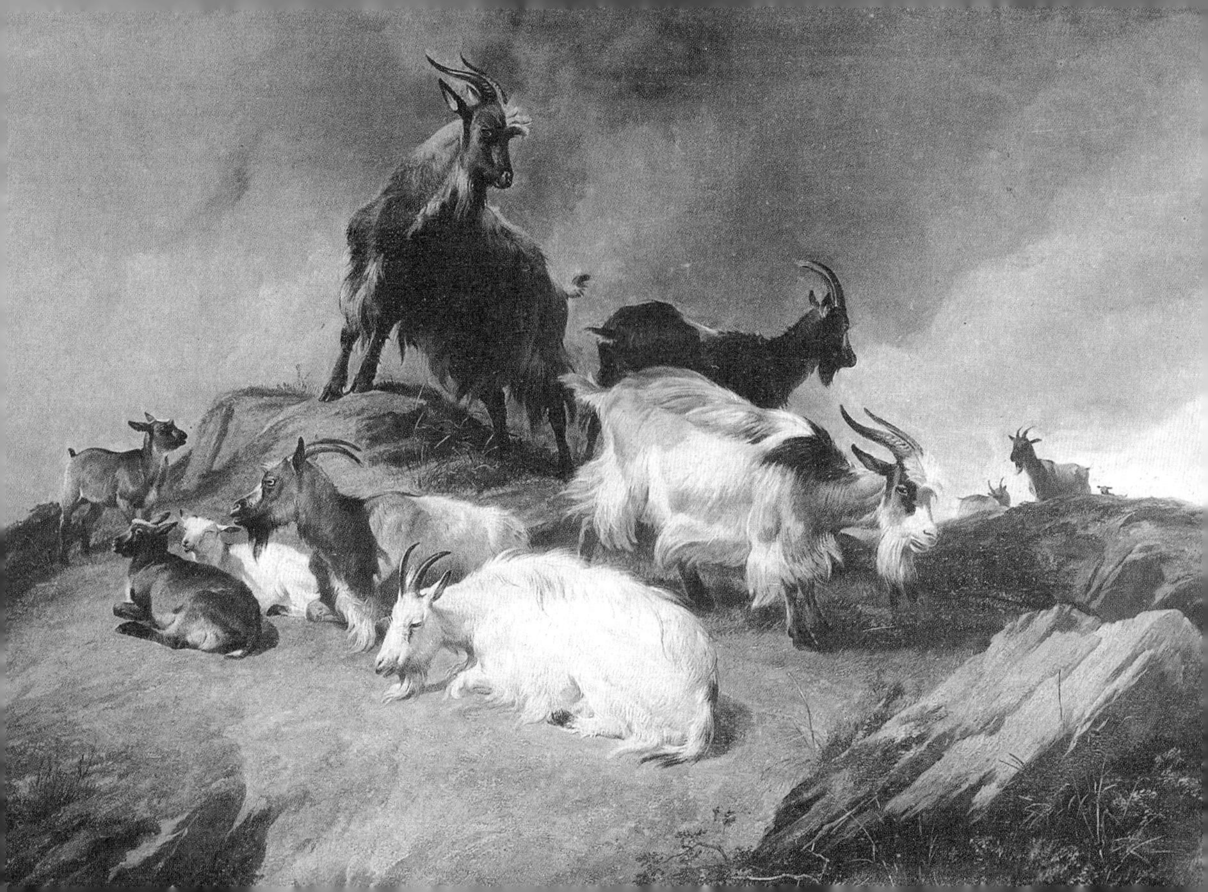

Chilled Avocado Soup

*A pretty-coloured and deliciously creamy soup with lots of flavour.
As the flesh of the avocados discolours rapidly, in spite of the lemon juice,
only make this soup on the day it is to be eaten.*

**3 avocados   2 cloves garlic, crushed   1½ tablespoons lemon juice
Salt and black pepper   1 pint approx. chicken stock
1 large pot thick and creamy Greek yoghurt
Chopped fresh parsley or mint to garnish**

Make sure the avocados are ripe but not over-ripe. Cut them in half, twist and remove the stones and scrape out all the flesh from the skins. Roughly chop the flesh. Put the garlic, lemon juice and salt and pepper into a liquidiser and add about half the chicken stock with the chopped avocado flesh. Blend for about 10 to 15 seconds and pour the contents into a soup tureen. Then stir in the yoghurt and the remaining chicken stock until it is well mixed. Chill in the refrigerator for several hours before serving. Serve garnished with a little chopped parsley or mint on each portion. Serves 4 to 6.

Up on the Mountain by Thomas Sidney Cooper RA

Garlicky Mushroom Ramekins

*This dish makes a tasty and attractive starter, especially
if scallop shells can be substituted for ramekins.*

**1 large onion, chopped   2 cloves of garlic, crushed
10 oz button mushrooms, roughly chopped   2 oz butter
2 oz Cheddar cheese, grated   Sprigs of fresh parsley to garnish**

SAUCE

2 oz butter   2 oz plain flour   1 pint milk   Salt and black pepper

Melt the butter in a saucepan, add the chopped onion and mushrooms and the garlic and cook gently until softened; remove from the heat. Make the white sauce in another saucepan. Melt the butter, stir in the flour and cook gently for 1 minute. Add the milk slowly, over a gentle heat, stirring all the time until the sauce thickens. Season with salt and pepper. Tip the contents of one saucepan into the other and stir well together. Divide the mixture into buttered ramekins or shells, sprinkle with grated cheese and place under a hot grill to melt the cheese and brown the tops. Garnish with sprigs of parsley and serve piping hot with a salad and fresh granary rolls. Serves about 6 to 8.

Cheese Scones

*These scones are quick and easy to make and are delicious eaten while still warm.
If yoghurt is not available, use milk or sour milk as a substitute.*

**8 oz self-raising flour
½ teaspoon English mustard powder
A pinch of salt
2 oz butter, softened
A few chopped chives (optional)
3 oz Cheddar cheese, grated
2-3 tablespoons yoghurt**

Set oven to 400°F or Mark 6. Butter a baking sheet. Sieve the flour, mustard powder and salt into a bowl and rub in the butter. If using chives, add them now. Add the grated cheese and mix to a soft dough with sufficient of the yoghurt. Roll out the mixture to about 1 inch thickness on a floured surface and cut out into circles with a pastry cutter (or a tumbler). Arrange the scones on the baking sheet and bake for about 10 minutes until risen and slightly browned. Transfer to a wire rack to cool. Eat warm, split in half and spread with butter.

Banana Yoghurt Smoothie

This recipe makes a lovely smooth, nutritious drink. Other fruits may be substituted for banana. Strawberry and raspberry Smoothies not only taste delicious but look attractive too. Sugar may be used instead of honey. Experiment to find which flavours you like best.

1 pint ewes' milk yoghurt or thick and creamy Greek yoghurt
2 peeled bananas 1 tablespoon runny honey
Ground cinnamon for sprinkling

Put the yoghurt, bananas and honey into a blender and whiz up until smooth. Pour into tall glasses and sprinkle with ground cinnamon. Transform the Smoothie into a tasty breakfast cereal by adding toasted crunchy oats, chopped dates or dried fruit; the opportunities are endless.

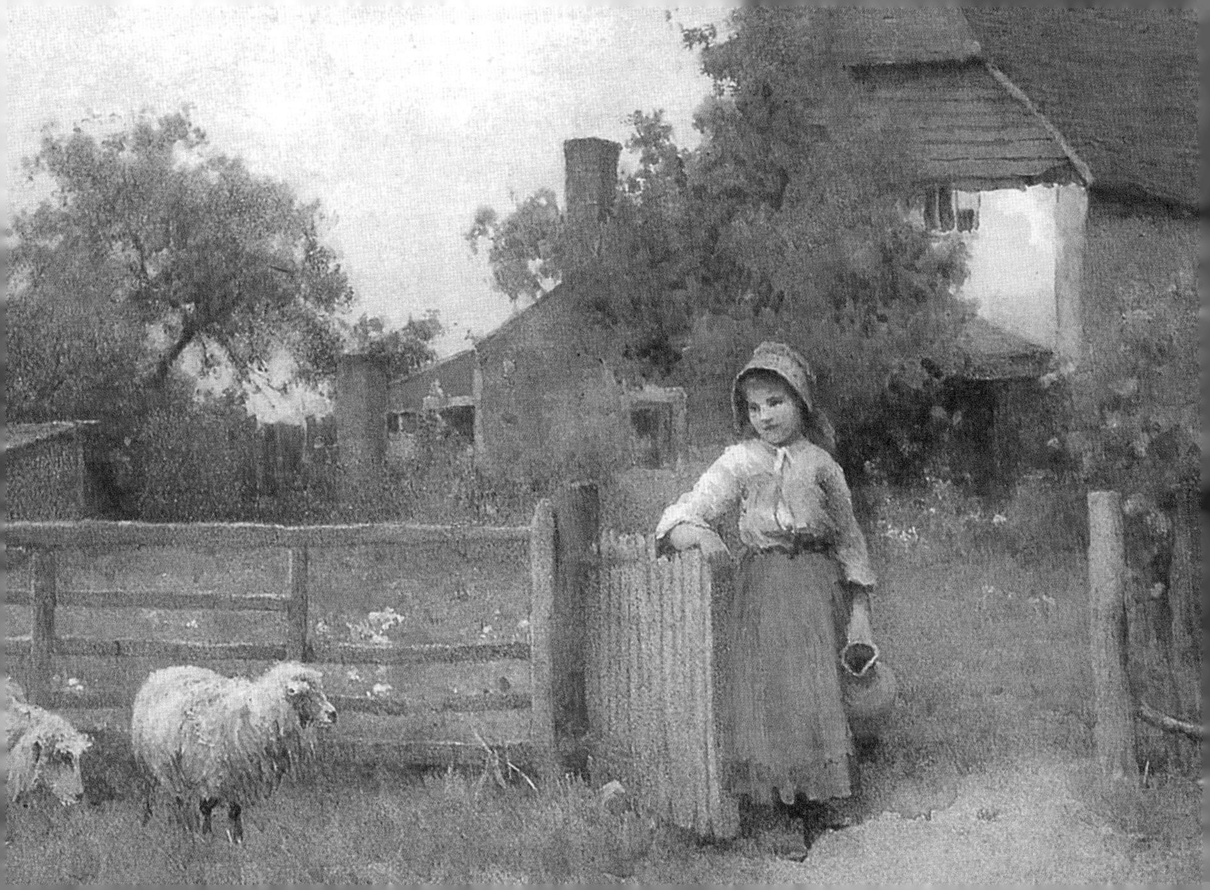

Cottage Cheese Tart

A delightful old country recipe that tastes delicious.

8 oz shortcrust pastry	**1 tablespoon rum or brandy (optional)**
2 oz butter	**2 tablespoons single cream**
12 oz cottage cheese	**Pinch of ground mixed spice**
3 oz caster sugar	**2½ oz currants or raisins**
2 eggs	**Grated nutmeg**

Set oven to 350°F or Mark 4. Butter an 8 to 9 inch flan dish. Roll out the pastry on a floured surface and line the dish. Trim the edge. Prick the base with a fork and bake blind for about 10 minutes. Leave to cool. Cream together the butter, cheese and sugar until smooth, then beat in the eggs, rum or brandy (if using), cream and mixed spice. Stir in the currants or raisins and put the mixture into the pastry case. Grate a little nutmeg over the top, reduce the oven temperature to 325°F or Mark 3 and bake for 40 minutes. Serve warm or cold. Serves 4 to 6.

Spinach Soup

This creamy summer soup used to be made with sorrel leaves before spinach was introduced into Britain in the 16th century. It is very nutritious and has lots of flavour.

About 1 lb spinach	**Cornflour for thickening**
A little butter	**½ pint thick yoghurt**
1-2 onions, chopped	**Salt and black pepper**
2 cloves garlic, crushed	**Grated nutmeg**
1 pint chicken stock	**Yoghurt to swirl**

First wash the spinach very well. Melt the butter in a large saucepan and gently cook the onion and garlic until soft. Shake excess water from the spinach, tear up the leaves and add to the pan. Cover and cook gently over a low heat for a few minutes until the spinach has cooked down. Add the chicken stock, transfer to a blender or food processor and whiz to liquidize. Return to the pan with a little slaked cornflour to thicken. Now add the yoghurt and stir constantly over a low heat until the soup has thickened. Season with salt and freshly ground black pepper and a generous grating of nutmeg. Serve hot, but not boiling, with a swirl of yoghurt in each bowl. Serves 4.

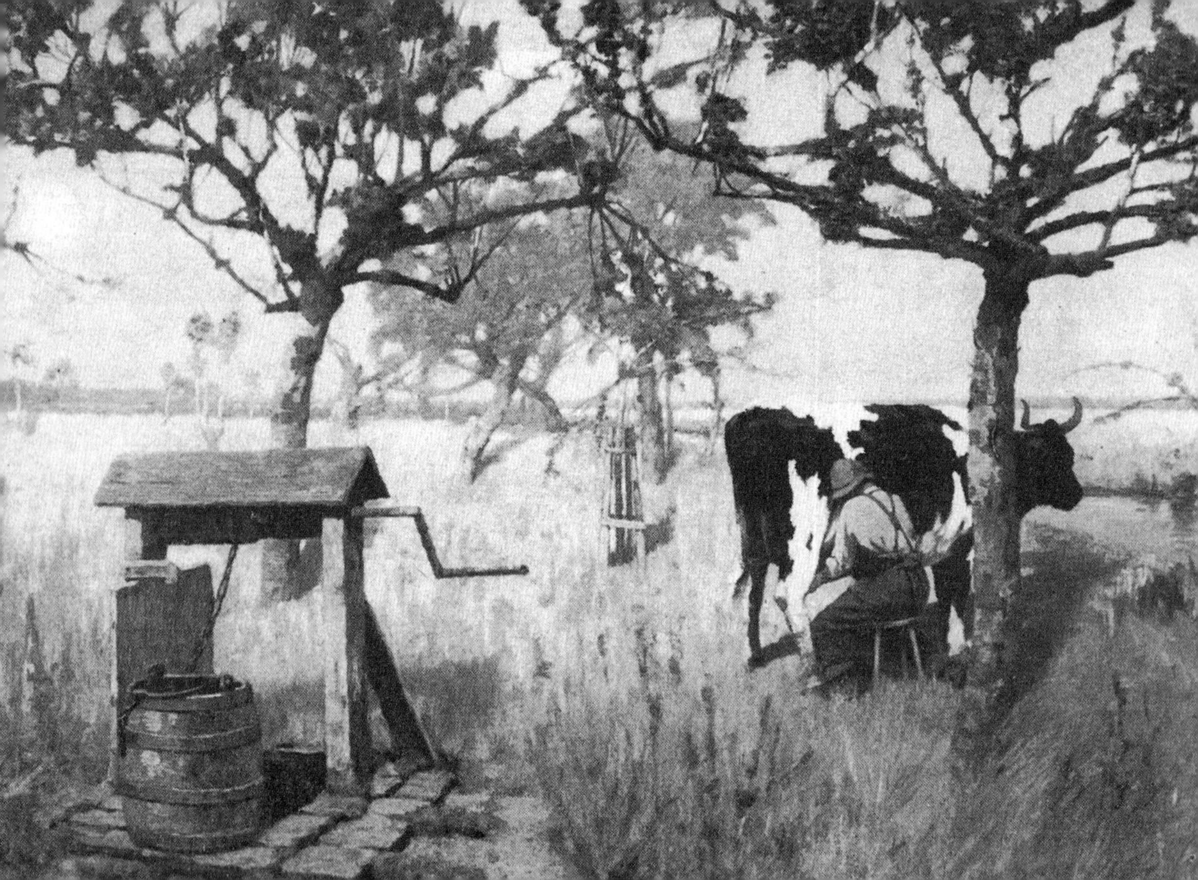

Cheese, Tomato & Bacon Flan

Cheese flans in various forms make a versatile satisfying dish which tastes as good eaten cold as hot. Smoked bacon would add to the flavour, if preferred.

8 oz shortcrust pastry
6 oz streaky bacon, cut into pieces
1 large onion, roughly chopped
1 clove garlic, crushed
Cooking oil

2 eggs, beaten
¼ pint milk
Freshly ground black pepper
2 oz Cheddar cheese, grated
2 tomatoes, sliced into wheels

A sprinkling of oregano or basil

Set oven to 375°F or Mark 5. Butter a 9 inch flan dish. Roll out the pastry on a floured surface and line the dish. Trim the edge. Prick the pastry all over with a fork and bake blind for about 10 minutes. Meanwhile, heat a little oil in a frying pan and fry the bacon and onion together with the garlic until the bacon is cooked and the onion is soft but not brown. Arrange the bacon, onion and garlic over the pastry base. In a jug, mix the beaten eggs with the milk and some twists of pepper and stir in half of the grated cheese. Pour the mixture over the flan filling. Arrange the tomato wheels over the top and sprinkle over the remaining grated cheese with a little oregano or basil. Bake for about 25 minutes until the topping is set. Serves 4 to 6.

Milking Time by John Miller

Cheese Pudding

This light, soufflé-like cheese pudding makes a tasty and surprisingly filling high-tea dish.

2 eggs, separated   ½ pint milk   1 oz butter
A good pinch of English mustard powder
3 oz fresh breadcrumbs
4 oz Cheddar cheese, grated   Salt and pepper

Set oven to 350°F or Mark 4. Butter a pie dish. Separate the eggs and beat the yolks lightly in a mixing bowl. Warm the milk and add to the eggs, together with the butter and good pinch of mustard powder. Mix well and stir in the breadcrumbs and most of the cheese. Season with salt and pepper. Whip the egg whites stiffly and fold into the mixture. Pour the mixture into the dish and sprinkle over the remaining grated cheese. Cook for 30 to 40 minutes until well risen, golden brown and just set in the middle. Serve with buttered crusty bread. Serves 4.

Cauliflower, Broccoli, Cheese & Tomato Bake

A simple-to-make and nutritious lunch or supper dish.

**A few cauliflower florets   A few broccoli heads   1 large onion, chopped
1 clove garlic, crushed   A knob of butter   6 tomatoes
3 oz Cheddar cheese, grated   Freshly torn leaves of basil**

SAUCE: 2 oz plain flour   2 oz butter   1 pint milk   Salt   Black pepper

Set oven to 350°F or Mark 4. Butter a shallow ovenproof dish. Wash the cauliflower and broccoli florets and steam or boil until just cooked. The broccoli should still be bright green. Melt the butter in a saucepan and cook the onion and garlic over a low heat until soft. When cooked put into the dish with the cauliflower and broccoli. Skin 5 of the 6 tomatoes by plunging them in boiling water and then peel. Chop the tomatoes roughly and add to the vegetables in the dish. Make the sauce. Melt the butter in a pan, stir in the flour and cook for 1 minute. Add the milk a little at a time, stirring continuously over a low heat to make a thickish sauce. Season with salt and pepper and stir in half the cheese and some basil leaves. Pour the sauce over the vegetables in the dish. Cut the last tomato into wheels and arrange over the top. Sprinkle over the rest of the cheese. Bake for about 15 minutes until browned on top, and garnish with basil leaves. Serves 4.

METRIC CONVERSIONS

The weights, measures and oven temperatures used in the preceding recipes can be easily converted to their metric equivalents. The conversions listed below are only approximate, having been rounded up or down as may be appropriate.

Weights

Avoirdupois	Metric
1 oz.	just under 30 grams
4 oz. (¼ lb.)	app. 115 grams
8 oz. (½ lb.)	app. 230 grams
1 lb.	454 grams

Liquid Measures

Imperial	Metric
1 tablespoon (liquid only)	20 millilitres
1 fl. oz.	app. 30 millilitres
1 gill (¼ pt.)	app. 145 millilitres
½ pt.	app. 285 millilitres
1 pt.	app. 570 millilitres
1 qt.	app. 1.140 litres

Oven Temperatures

	°Fahrenheit	Gas Mark	°Celsius
Slow	300	2	150
	325	3	170
Moderate	350	4	180
	375	5	190
	400	6	200
Hot	425	7	220
	450	8	230
	475	9	240

Flour as specified in these recipes refers to plain flour unless otherwise described.